MOUNT VERNON

MOUNT VERNON

Maxwell Macmillan Canada
Toronto
Maxwell Macmillan International
New York   Oxford   Singapore   Sydney

by Catherine Reef

DILLON PRESS
New York

Photo Credits

James Blank: front cover; Kendrick Photography: back cover; Kendrick Photography: pages 2-3, 10, 30 (top and bottom), 36 (bottom), 41, 51, 63; National Gallery of Art: 12; The Mount Vernon Ladies' Association: 18, 26, 36 (top), 39, 44, 46, 48, 54 (top and bottom), 56, 64

Library of Congress Cataloging-in-Publication Data

Reef, Catherine.
    Mount Vernon / Catherine Reef.
      p. cm. — (Places in American history)
    Summary: Presents a history of George Washington's home, as it was when he lived there to its current status as a historic site.
    ISBN 0-87518-474-X
      1. Mount Vernon (Va. : Estate)—Juvenile literature. 2. Washington, George, 1732-1799—Homes and haunts—Virginia—Fairfax County—Juvenile literature. [1. Mount Vernon (Va.: Estate) 2. Washington, George, 1732-1799—Homes and haunts.] I. Title. II. Series.
E842.9.R33   1992
973.4'1'092—dc20   91-33494

Copyright © 1992 by Dillon Press, Macmillan Publishing Company

All rights reserved. No part of this book may be reproduced or transmitted in any form or by any means, electronic or mechanical, including photocopying, recording, or by any information storage and retrieval system, without permission in writing from the Publisher.

Dillon Press   Maxwell Macmillan Canada, Inc.
Macmillan Publishing Company   1200 Eglinton Avenue East
866 Third Avenue   Suite 200
New York, NY 10022   Don Mills, Ontario M3C 3N1

Macmillan Publishing Company is part of the Maxwell Communication Group of Companies.

First edition

Printed in the United States of America
10 9 8 7 6 5 4 3 2 1

CONTENTS

1. George Washington's Home................................. 7

2. A Soldier's House................................14

3. Family Man................................23

4. Equal to the Command................................32

5. Mount Vernon's Rebirth................................42

6. Mount Vernon: Step Inside................................53

Mount Vernon: A Historical Time Line................66

Visitor Information................................70

Index................................71

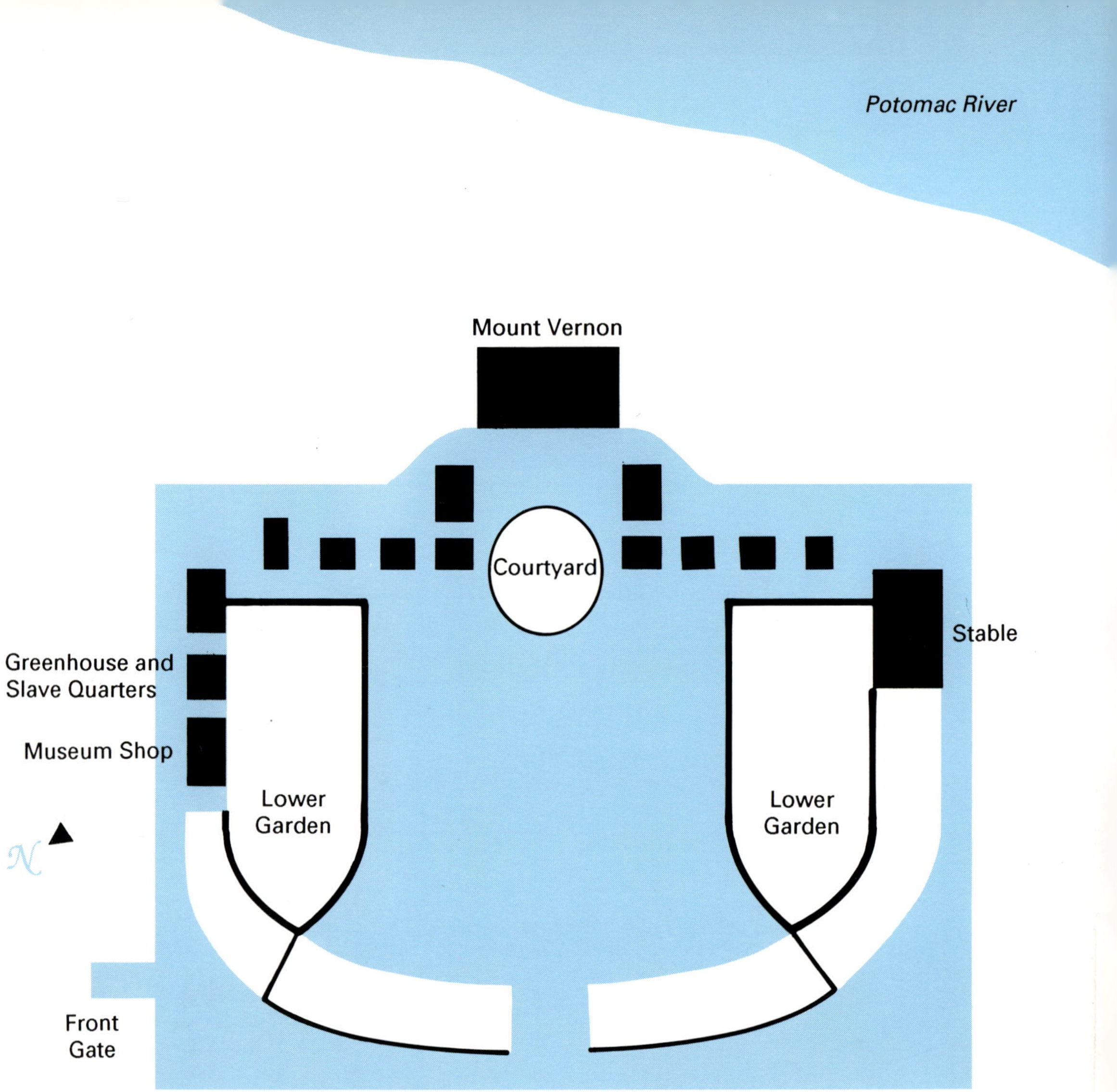

Potomac River

Mount Vernon

Courtyard

Greenhouse and
Slave Quarters

Museum Shop

Stable

Lower Garden

Lower Garden

N

Front Gate

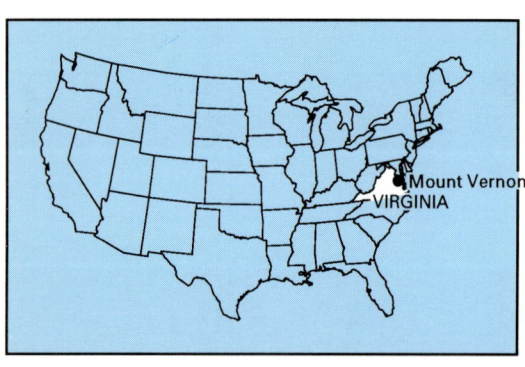

Mount Vernon
VIRGINIA

CHAPTER 1

George Washington's Home

June had not yet arrived, but already a muggy haze rose from the Potomac River. On that warm day in 1752, 20-year-old George Washington sat on a high, grassy riverbank.

Brushing a mosquito away from his face, the young man wished that he could see beyond the river and the great Chesapeake Bay into which it flowed. He wished that he could travel swiftly from the Virginia Colony to the island of Bermuda. There, off the North Carolina coast, George longed to see his half brother, Lawrence.

Lawrence had come down with tuberculosis, a disease that attacks the lungs. He hoped that Bermuda's warm, sunny climate would make him well. But Lawrence's last letter had not sounded hopeful. "If I grow worse," he'd written, "I shall hurry home to my grave."

George had spent much of his youth at Lawrence's home, Mount Vernon. Lawrence had fought with the British navy. As George listened to Lawrence's tales of battle, he decided that he, too, would like to be a soldier or sailor. George missed Lawrence's exciting stories and hoped that he would soon grow well.

But Lawrence did not get well. He returned to Mount Vernon in worse health than when he left, and died in July of 1752.

Within months of Lawrence's death, George began a military career of his own, fighting with the British army against the French for the ownership of western lands. He proved to be a brave and skillful fighter in the wilderness.

When the American colonists fought against England in the war for independence, they chose George Washington as the commander of their Continental army. Washington quickly took control of this new, untrained military force and led it to victory.

However, George Washington is not called the "father" of his country simply because he was an outstanding military leader. He also did much to shape the government of his new nation, the United States of America. When American statesmen met to draft the Constitution, the document that was to be the framework of their government and laws, George Washington presided. And because they so greatly admired him, his fellow citizens elected George Washington the first president of the United States.

As busy as he was, George Washington valued home and family life. Soon after Lawrence's death, he made Mount Vernon his home. He enlarged his brother's small house in the hope of raising a family there. Although George Washington never had children of his own, the children and grandchildren of his wife, Martha, grew up on the estate.

At Mount Vernon, George Washington tried out new farming methods. In the details of his house and grounds, he expressed his ideas on beauty and design.

Washington was loved in his day as both a leader and a friend. He was "first in war, first in peace, first in the hearts of his countrymen," one of his generals said. In the years since Washington's death, Americans have continued to honor his memory. They gave his name to one of the 50 states and to the nation's capital. In that capital, Washington, D.C., a white stone monument to George Washington stands 555 feet (169 meters) high, taller than any other structure in the city.

Another memorial to George Washington stands proudly on the banks of the Potomac River. It is Mount Vernon, older than the United States itself. The house, grounds, and outbuildings have been restored to look as they did in 1799, the year Washington died. The mansion's rooms hold furniture, dishes, books, and other

Visitors at the gate to the bowling green

items that the Washington family used. The orderly gardens contain flowers, herbs, and vegetables such as those grown in Washington's time. In the service buildings are tools such as those used by Mount Vernon's slaves and servants.

Each year, more than one million visitors walk along Mount Vernon's tree-lined lanes. They tour the rooms where Washington joined his family for meals or music or spent time alone in quiet study. Everywhere, they gaze upon scenes that George Washington loved: the lush woods on the far side of the Potomac River, sunlight streaming through a pasture fence, a child's harpsichord in a parlor corner.

At Mount Vernon, as nowhere else, people come to understand George Washington the man.

A Washington family portrait. George and his wife, Martha, are seated, while Martha's grandchildren, George Washington Parke Custis and Nelly Custis, stand.

CHAPTER 2

A Soldier's House

Many people who visit Mount Vernon feel that they are looking back in time. As they walk through the three-story mansion or stand on the long, columned porch, they imagine that it is the late 18th century. The scenes they see are the same ones that George Washington looked upon.

But if these people could look further back in time, they would see a smaller, simpler house on this site. In 1735, Augustine and Mary Washington settled in that small house, on a farm called Little Hunting Creek Plantation. Their son George, born on February 22, 1732, was just three years old.

When George was six years old, he met the best friend he would ever have. His half brother

Lawrence had just returned from school in England. Twenty-year-old Lawrence had picked up fine manners at school, but his friendliness and interest in George came naturally.

Soon Lawrence left again—to join the British navy. England had gone to war with Spain over the right to trade with Spain's American colonies. George waited eagerly for Lawrence's letters from the Caribbean, which could take up to four months to arrive. Lawrence's news often brought the family more worry than comfort. "The enemy killed of ours some 600 and some wounded and the climate killed us in greater number," Lawrence wrote after one battle.

George did not always have time to worry about Lawrence, though. His schooling had begun. Now living with his family at Ferry Farm, another Virginia site, George studied mathematics, astronomy, and other subjects, getting ready for school in England.

But when George was 11 years old, his plans

suddenly changed. Augustine Washington died, leaving George and his mother to manage Ferry Farm. An English education was out of the question—George's mother needed him at home. Grieving and disappointed, the boy helped his mother tend the tobacco crop and supervise the family's slaves.

One fact, at least, brought George happiness. Lawrence was home from the war. George slipped away from his hard work whenever he could to visit Lawrence and his new wife, Anne, at the Little Hunting Creek Plantation. Lawrence had inherited the farm when his father died. He had renamed it Mount Vernon, after the English admiral Edward Vernon, a man he greatly admired. Lawrence had served under Admiral Vernon in the West Indies, and the two had become friends.

Life at Mount Vernon gave George many opportunities to learn. He attended parties and learned to dance well. Lawrence taught him to hunt and fish. George learned to love horses and became an excellent rider. He listened to Lawrence's exciting war stories and thought that he, too, might one day see battle.

Lawrence encouraged George to join the navy, but Mary Washington did not want her son to fight in wars. She approved of another profession, however. George had learned surveying—the science of measuring land. A surveyor's life might lack the excitement of a sailor's, but it could be a way to explore the unknown West.

At Mount Vernon, George met Lord Fairfax, a wealthy relative of Anne's. Lord Fairfax owned a great deal of land in Virginia and was known as an odd character. He bought trunks full of new clothes, yet wore the same old ones day after day. He disliked many people.

But Lord Fairfax took a liking to George. The tall 16-year-old with reddish hair exhibited intelligence and good sense. Lord Fairfax had planned an expedition to survey some of his

18 ✪ MOUNT VERNON

land. He invited George to go along.

For the first time, George traveled beyond the Blue Ridge Mountains to the raw and beautiful Shenandoah Valley. He encountered a rattlesnake and rode his horse across a swiftly flowing river. George and his companions hunted for food and often slept on the ground.

One night, the group stayed at a country inn. Its poor quality came as a surprise to George. "I, not being as good a woodsman as the rest of my company, stripped myself very orderly and went in to bed," he wrote. The bed's worn blanket, George soon learned, contained "double its weight of vermin, such as lice, fleas, etc." Quickly George put on his clothes and slept with his companions on the floor.

George continued to work as a surveyor in the years ahead. He helped to measure the land for a new town on the Potomac River near Alexandria, Virginia. He surveyed again in the Shenandoah Valley and bought land of his own.

A view of Mount Vernon, painted about 1792

George's surveying career halted in 1751, when Lawrence became ill with tuberculosis. Lawrence believed that a tropical climate might help to heal his lungs. He asked George, now 19, to travel with him to Barbados, an island in the West Indies.

In Barbados, illness struck George as well. He caught smallpox, a contagious disease that killed many people in the 18th century. George was strong enough to survive. But smallpox causes scabs to form on the body, and George was left with a scarred face.

While George returned to Virginia, Lawrence moved on to Bermuda. Lawrence was too ill to benefit from sunshine and warm air, however. He returned home to die in the summer of 1752.

Lawrence had served as adjutant general before getting sick. It had been his job to train Virginia's volunteer militia, or army. Now, Lawrence's death left that position empty. George decided to take Lawrence's place. Just weeks before his 21st birthday, he was granted the position and became Major George Washington.

The young major drilled the militia in fighting skills—skills he had to learn from books. But soon he had more important concerns. French troops were building forts along Lake Erie, on land that the English considered their own. The problem was, the French claimed it, too.

Washington took part in the battles that followed, as the English and French fought for the land. Now a colonel, he commanded a group of volunteer soldiers who built a fort, called Fort Necessity, on the Ohio River. When the French attacked Fort Necessity, the soldiers from England and the colonies bravely fought back.

After fighting for hours in a rainstorm, Washington's men had wet gunpowder and no food. One-third of them were dead or wounded. Sadly, Washington surrendered Fort Necessity to the French. He marched his worn-out troops back to Virginia.

The colonial leaders hailed Washington as a hero. He had fought bravely, they said, although the French had outnumbered his men. But Washington did not receive a promotion for his bravery. Instead, the governor told him that England was lowering the ranks of all colonial officers. Angry at this unfair treatment, Washington resigned.

Out of the army, Washington needed a place to live. He could have settled with his mother at Ferry Farm. But at age 22, he wanted a home of his own. Lawrence's widow, Anne, had remarried, and Mount Vernon now stood vacant. George rented the estate from her for 15,000 pounds (5,600 kilograms) of tobacco a year.

George Washington missed the soldier's life. As he put it, "My inclinations are strongly bent to arms." Yet as he stood in the empty rooms where he had listened, years earlier, to Lawrence's war stories, he felt he truly had come home.

CHAPTER 3

Family Man

Living alone at Mount Vernon, George Washington thought about the future. He hoped to marry and, one day, see his children running through the grass and trees. With the hope of raising a family, he added a third story to his home.

Washington also wanted Mount Vernon's farmland to provide the greatest yield. At first he raised tobacco, the most common crop in Virginia. Most of the tobacco was exported to England, but tobacco prices fell. Then Washington tried growing several other plants at Mount Vernon, and soon settled on wheat as his main crop. The wheat grew easily and well. It could be sold and milled into flour right there in Virginia.

Always eager to try new farming methods,

Washington experimented with crop rotation. Every few years, he grew new crops in certain fields. Because each crop needed different amounts of various nutrients, this practice helped to keep the soil rich.

 Washington did not turn his back on soldiering altogether. The French and Indian War was raging, as England fought with France for control of territory in the New World. In 1755, General Edward Braddock asked for Washington's help. Braddock was leading a troop of soldiers 90 miles (145 kilometers) into the wilderness to attack the French. Braddock wanted Washington, with his knowledge of the woodlands, to serve as a guide.

 Washington had resigned from the army in anger, but he accepted Braddock's offer. It was a chance to learn fighting tactics from an experienced general. But Washington soon learned that the European style of fighting did not work well in the New World. Used to battling in open fields, the British soldiers did not know how to fight in the woods. Following a surprise attack by the French and Indians, the English soldiers "broke and ran as sheep before hounds," Washington wrote.

Braddock, wounded in the shoulder and chest, died three days later. "I luckily escaped without a wound," Washington wrote, "though I had four bullets through my coat and two horses shot under me."

After Braddock's death, the 23-year-old Washington was appointed commander of all of Virginia's troops. He led Virginia's forces for three and a half years, until he was elected to the House of Burgesses, Virginia's governing body, and resigned his post in the service.

At Mount Vernon and in the colonial capital, Williamsburg, Washington enjoyed the pleasant life of a Virginia country gentleman. He rode in fox hunts and danced at parties and balls. One of his dancing partners was a small, plump,

pretty woman named Martha Custis. Martha's husband had recently died, leaving her one of the wealthiest women in Virginia. She had a son and a daughter, named Jacky and Patsy.

Martha and George became good friends, and were married on January 6, 1759. The family lived for a short time in Williamsburg, where George continued to serve in the House of Burgesses. In April of 1759, George, Martha, and the children settled at Mount Vernon.

Washington inherited Mount Vernon in 1761, when Lawrence's widow, Anne, died. At last the home was truly his own. And although he still served in the House of Burgesses, Washington gave most of his attention to home and family life.

As the children grew up, Washington planned to enlarge Mount Vernon even more. His plans called for an addition to each end of the house— a large dining room at one end and a study and master bedroom at the other. Washington had many ideas for improving Mount Vernon, based

George and Martha Washington, painted by Charles Willson Peale

on books he had read about country homes in England and fine houses he had seen in Williamsburg. He planned for a long, columned porch, or piazza; grand formal gardens; and a bowling green—a long, well-tended lawn.

The house was to be covered with "rusticated boards," planks of wood that were cut to resemble blocks of stone. Sand added to the paint gave the boards a rough texture.

Mount Vernon also needed new and larger outbuildings, Washington decided. In the kitchen, washhouse, stable, and other service buildings, slaves did much of the work necessary to run the large estate. Like many Southern planters, Washington depended on slave labor. Yet he opposed the practice of slavery. "I am principled against this kind of traffic in the human species," he wrote. And unlike most other planters, he freed his slaves in his will.

Once the work began, Washington supervised every aspect of the project. "It's astonishing with what niceness he directs everything in the building way," commented a guest. Washington even did all of the measuring himself, noted the guest, so "that all may be perfectly uniform."

Life at Mount Vernon kept Washington busy. But events were happening throughout the colonies, events too exciting to ignore.

The colonists had become tired of the many taxes they had to pay to England. England taxed them on everything from legal documents to glass and tea. In protest, the colonists organized boycotts. They refused to buy English goods, hoping to force England into repealing the taxes.

Many colonists wanted to be free of more than English taxes. They wanted to be free of English government as well. Washington realized that the struggle for liberty might involve war. "No man should scruple, or hesitate a moment to use arms in defense of so valuable a blessing," he wrote.

At last, Washington could no longer stay at

home and concentrate on building. In September of 1774, he traveled to Philadelphia, Pennsylvania, to join a group of colonial leaders called the Continental Congress. This group called upon King George III of England to protect the colonists' rights.

The king ignored their plea, however. And when the Continental Congress met again in 1775, American and British soldiers had exchanged gunfire in Boston and on a bridge in Concord, Massachusetts. The war for independence had begun.

The Continental Congress decided to raise an army for the war. When it came time to choose a commander, everyone present voted for the same person: George Washington, who knew well how to fight in the wilderness. Washington accepted the post but warned the others, "I do not think myself equal to the command."

Above: the piazza at Mount Vernon overlooking the Potomac River
Below: the slave quarters at Mount Vernon

CHAPTER 4

Equal to the Command

For eight long years, Washington missed the comforts of home. He and his army rarely had enough food, clothing, or ammunition. The soldiers sometimes marched barefoot in the snow. Many deserted, or left their posts, risking severe punishment. But Washington quickly proved that he was "equal to the command." He stayed close to his soldiers and shared many of their hardships. He soon became a hero to many Americans.

Martha spent the winters in camp with her husband and his soldiers. She left Mount Vernon at the end of autumn and returned in the spring, as the soldiers marched off to battle.

Washington depended on reports from his

cousin, Lund Washington, for news of Mount Vernon. Lund supervised the building of the new additions while Washington was away, and once he saved the estate from attack.

A British warship had anchored in the Potomac River, and its sailors demanded food from Lund. Fearing they would destroy Mount Vernon, Lund gave the sailors food and drink. News of this event made Washington furious. He would have preferred to hear that Lund had refused the sailors' request, he wrote, even if "they had burnt my House, and laid the Plantation in ruins."

The long fight between the Americans and the British ended in 1781, when Lord Cornwallis of England surrendered to Washington in Yorktown, Virginia. The English and Americans signed a treaty in 1783, and Washington resigned from the army. Some of his officers wanted to make Washington their king, but he desired no part of that plan. "Banish these thoughts from your mind," he told them.

The 51-year-old Washington retired to Mount Vernon on Christmas Eve. Once more, he devoted his energy to home and family life. He supervised the work on his bowling green, helping to reshape the slope of the land and transplanting trees and bushes from the nearby woods. He ordered stone for his piazza floor from England. Washington also renewed his experiments in farming. He tried more new crops and crop-rotation systems.

George and Martha Washington entertained many guests at Mount Vernon—so many that Washington called his home "a well resorted tavern." The couple also continued to care for two children. Martha's son, Jacky, had died in 1781. The Washingtons took in his youngest children, Nelly Custis and George Washington Parke Custis, and raised them at Mount Vernon.

After a few years of quiet retirement, however, Washington again returned to Philadelphia and public life. In 1787, he served as president of the Constitutional Convention, the meeting to draft the United States Constitution.

Over a long and very hot summer, the convention delegates created the framework of the United States government. They organized the Congress, the government's lawmaking body. They planned for the Supreme Court, the highest court to which people can turn for a legal decision. They also decided that a president would be elected to lead the nation and see that Congress's laws were carried out. The delegates held strong opinions on the kind of government that would be best, and they often disagreed. "To please all is impossible," Washington wrote.

In September, the Constitutional Convention at last finished its work. It was now up to the states to approve the new Constitution. George Washington went home to Mount Vernon and completed another project. He added the finishing touch to his remodeled home—a weather

vane shaped like a dove of peace.

Again, however, Washington could not retire. On April 14, 1789, Secretary of Congress Charles Thomson arrived at Mount Vernon. He had traveled from Philadelphia, a trip that took several days. In the large dining room at Mount Vernon, Thomson gave George Washington some important news. Washington had been elected president of the United States.

It was a humble Washington who accepted the historic position. "I walk on untrodden ground," he said. As the first president, Washington could not follow in earlier leaders' footsteps. He had to make his own way as he led the American people.

The president needed to live in the capital, near the other members of government. New York City was the capital when Washington became president. He and Martha lived there until 1790, when Philadelphia became the capital. For the eight years of Washington's presi-

Above: the weather vane
Below: the little parlor at Mount Vernon, showing Nelly Custis's harpsichord

dency, the couple was only able to visit Mount Vernon occasionally.

President George Washington worked with Congress to shape the new government. Under President Washington, Congress created three government departments: the departments of foreign affairs, war, and the treasury. Congress also adopted the Bill of Rights. These ten amendments to the Constitution protect Americans' basic freedoms, such as freedom of speech and freedom of religion.

President Washington also chose the site for a new capital city, to be located on the Potomac River, just 12 miles (19 kilometers) north of Mount Vernon. He hired Pierre Charles L'Enfant, a French engineer, to design a grand city—known today as Washington, D.C.—on the piece of land that was 10 square miles (26 square kilometers).

In March of 1797, George Washington retired as president and returned to live at Mount

George and Martha Washington's bedchamber

Vernon. His responsibilities had aged him, and friends said he looked older than his 65 years.

Still, Washington's days began early. He rose each morning before sunrise to spend time alone in his study, planning the day's activities. At 7:00 A.M., he joined the household for breakfast. While the others ate cold and boiled meats, Washington enjoyed his favorite breakfast—three cakes of cornmeal mush "swimming in butter and honey," along with "three cups of tea without cream."

Washington made daily rides to his farms, and he continued to beautify his house and gardens. He supervised craftsmen as they gave Mount Vernon's pine woodwork a "mahogany finish," a surface painted to look like more expensive wood. He enlarged Mount Vernon's greenhouse and planted a thick hedge around his flower garden.

Mount Vernon's owner took daily horseback rides on his property, whatever the weather. On December 12, 1799, he rode for five hours in spite of the rain, snow, and sleet that fell all day. He awoke the next day with a sore throat, and by the 14th was so ill that Martha sent for a doctor.

Dr. James Craik found a patient who could barely speak. He called Washington's sore throat and high fever "inflammatory quinsy," but some modern doctors think that it was a strep throat. Craik could not offer Washington any treatment that helped, and the former president grew

Visitors at George Washington's tomb

weaker by the hour. "You had better not take any more trouble about me," Washington whispered late in the day. "I cannot last long."

Between 10:00 and 11:00 P.M., George Washington died. He was buried in the family vault at Mount Vernon. Martha Washington died two and one-half years later, in May of 1802.

CHAPTER 5

Mount Vernon's Rebirth

Mount Vernon passed from one family member to another after Martha Washington died.

John Augustine Washington, Jr., was the last family member to own Mount Vernon. By 1850, when he took possession of the estate, owning Mount Vernon had become a burden. The farms showed a poor profit, and the house suffered from neglect. What's more, many visitors came to the estate—most of them strangers. As new roads were built and steamboats carried passengers up and down the Potomac, more and more curious Americans came to see the first president's home.

John Augustine Washington, Jr., offered to sell Mount Vernon to the United States government so that it could be preserved as a historic site. But the government was not interested. The Commonwealth of Virginia did not want to buy the estate either.

The chain of events that saved Mount Vernon began with a nighttime boat ride in 1853. Louisa Cunningham of South Carolina stood on the deck of a steamboat as it traveled down the Potomac River. Like all seamen at that time, the steamboat's captain tolled the ship's bell as the vessel passed Mount Vernon.

Cunningham had visited Mount Vernon as a child. She remembered seeing a grand, white home with a lush lawn and well-tended gardens. But the building she saw on that moonlit night looked fallen-down and ghostly. The white paint was peeling from its walls, the roof sank in the middle, and one of the pillars supporting the porch had collapsed.

Cunningham felt ashamed that her country would allow Mount Vernon to fall into decay. She

Mount Vernon as it looked about 1858, before the restoration

expressed her feelings in a letter to her daughter, Ann Pamela. If the government would not preserve this historic place, Louisa Cunningham wrote, perhaps the American women should take on the job.

"I will do it!" said Ann Pamela Cunningham when she read her mother's letter. Immediately, the young woman wrote a letter to the *Charleston Mercury*, a local newspaper, urging women to give money to the cause. Restoring Mount Vernon "would save American honor from a blot in the eyes of a gazing world," she wrote. Soon newspapers throughout the country printed the letter.

Ann Pamela Cunningham next formed an

organization, the Mount Vernon Ladies' Association of the Union, to receive the contributions and purchase the estate. Edward Everett, one of the greatest speakers of his time, gave lectures to raise money for Mount Vernon. He raised more than $69,000 for the cause.

By December of 1858, the association had enough money to buy the house, the outbuildings, and 200 surrounding acres (81 hectares). Gifts of land would later increase the holdings to 500 acres (202 hectares). As soon as John Augustine Washington, Jr., moved out, the association set to work restoring the once-grand estate. They opened the doors to the public, charging 25 cents admission. Ann Pamela Cunningham hired Sarah Tracy, a young woman from Troy, New York, to work as her secretary.

The restoration work did not progress steadily, however. It was a time of trouble in the United States. For decades, people in the North and South had disagreed about the practice of

Washington's study

owning slaves in the South. As the dispute grew more intense, South Carolina seceded, or left the Union, in December of 1860. Ann Pamela Cunningham hurried home. The other Southern states followed South Carolina's example, and the Civil War, fought to reunite the nation, began in 1861.

Mount Vernon remained neutral ground during the war. The home of George Washington, leaders on both sides agreed, was too important to be spoiled by war. Sarah Tracy lived at Mount Vernon during the Civil War, which lasted until 1865. She often heard gunfire from the many battles that were fought in the surrounding countryside.

Ann Pamela Cunningham returned to Mount Vernon in 1866, and the restoration work began again. When Washington died, appraisers had made a complete inventory of Mount Vernon. They listed the contents of each room, as well as the tools used on Mount Vernon's farms. Those lists, along with Washington's letters, orders, and bills, helped the association restore Mount Vernon.

Acquiring furnishings that had been removed from the house turned out to be a long process, one that is still going on today. After Washington's death, Martha Washington gave many items away. In 1908, the descendants of George Washington Parke Custis returned the bed in which George Washington had died. It had stood for years at Arlington House, Custis's home in Virginia. A sketch that had been a gift to Washington from his friend the Marquis de

The West Parlor

Lafayette was discovered in a private collection in 1987. It is now on loan to Mount Vernon.

Some furnishings could not be found. In George Washington's day, for example, a group of chairs sat in a line on the piazza. Only one of those chairs remained. The chairs on the piazza today are copies of that original.

The association restored the house itself with the same attention to detail. To repair the piazza floor, they ordered stones from the quarry in England that had supplied the originals. They repainted the house using round brushes similar to those used in the 18th century.

Modern methods were used in the house, though, when they seemed to work best. For example, workers reinforced the structure with steel to give it strength. They coated the cornerstone with a chemical compound to prevent its deterioration.

The botanists who replanted Mount Vernon's gardens relied on some of Washington's own planting plans, his diary, and letters to replace the trees, vegetables, and herbs that he had planted. One letter mentioned a grove of locusts long since cut down. In 1934, gardeners planted a new grove of locusts on the spot.

When historical records do not exist, the association conducts research or turns to technology to learn about Mount Vernon's past. Archaeologists examined the site of Washington's greenhouse to gain information on its dimensions and construction. Archaeologists have also found clues in the soil about the way Mount Vernon's residents lived. Digging beneath the slaves' quarters, they recently found scraps of fine china, buttons, and buckles—evidence that the Washingtons may have passed on possessions to their slaves.

A computer aided the association members in 1980 when they wanted to learn what colors Washington had painted his interior walls. Over the years, those walls had been covered with many coats of paint. The computer analyzed data on paint chips from the walls to determine the exact shades Washington had used.

The preservation of Mount Vernon has extended beyond the house and grounds. In the 1950s, Frances P. Bolton, a member of the Mount Vernon Ladies' Association and a congresswoman from Ohio, learned that an oil company planned to build storage tanks across the river from Mount Vernon. Bolton could not bear to think that the view from Mount Vernon would be spoiled. She bought 750 acres (304 hectares) of land on the far shore to keep the riverbank

Washington's flower garden with the greenhouse in the background

green and natural. In 1974, that land became part of Piscataway National Park.

Restoring Mount Vernon has been a labor of love for many Americans, from Ann Pamela Cunningham to Frances P. Bolton to the people who work at Mount Vernon today. Each has helped to make Mount Vernon a place of beauty and pride on the broad American landscape.

CHAPTER 6

Mount Vernon: Step Inside

When King George VI of England visited the United States in 1939, his country was on the verge of war with Germany. Germany's Nazi army had invaded other countries in Europe, establishing strict control and taking away people's freedom.

Concerned about his nation's future, the king met with America's leaders. But he also found time to tour Mount Vernon. The first president's home reminded the king of values his nation and the United States shared: liberty and individual rights.

The king's daughter, Queen Elizabeth II, traveled to the United States in 1991. She, too, paid a call at the shrine of freedom. She became

one of the one million people who visit Mount Vernon each year.

As visitors approach Mount Vernon, they walk on paths alongside the bowling green, Washington's expansive, tree-lined lawn. They pass through the courtyard, where horse-drawn coaches once pulled up to Washington's door. They take a quick look at the sundial standing at the courtyard's center. They see the colonnades, columned shelters covering the walkways that lead from the mansion to two service buildings. They glance at the rusticated boards that cover the mansion's outside walls.

When people enter Washington's large dining room, the first thing they notice is its color. The walls have been painted a bright, bold shade called verdigris green that matches the original color. In this historic room, Washington learned he was elected president of the United States. In 1799, after he died, his body lay in this room for three days before burial.

Above: In 1939 King George VI and Queen Elizabeth of England visited Mount Vernon. Below: In 1991, their daughter, Queen Elizabeth II, came to the historic site.

Many people are surprised to see that this room contains no dining table. The Washingtons often used the large dining room for purposes other than eating. If they wanted to serve a meal, they asked their servants to set up tables made of trestles and boards. Washington had used this type of makeshift table while fighting in the Revolutionary War.

Two smaller rooms, the west parlor and the little parlor, adjoin the large dining room. The west parlor's walls are Prussian blue. Rich carvings over the fireplace and doorways give this room an elegant look. Many family portraits hang on the walls. A Chinese porcelain tea set sits on a table, along with a silver tray and urn. The Washingtons used these items to entertain their guests.

With its plain woodwork and simple furniture, the little parlor looks like a place for casual family gatherings. The cross-stitched cushions in this room are reproductions of a set that Martha

The large dining room

Washington made. Visitors can imagine the Washingtons sitting in this room listening to Nelly, Martha's granddaughter, play her harpsichord. Nelly took the harpsichord with her in 1802, when she moved from Mount Vernon. Her daughter-in-law returned it in 1859.

At the center of the house, running from front to back, is a wide, dark-paneled passage. Breezes make the passage a cool room in warm weather, and the Washingtons sometimes gathered there on hot, humid summer days.

A small case holding a key hangs on one wall in the passage. That key once opened the door to France's Bastille, an infamous prison. Crowds of French people destroyed the Bastille in 1789, at the start of the French Revolution. They set free seven prisoners, who had been held there unjustly.

Washington received the key from the Marquis de Lafayette, a French hero who had fought for American independence. Lafayette had become a close friend and admirer of Washington. In presenting the key, he wrote, "It is a tribute which I owe as a son to my adoptive father."

Many people feel closest to Washington when they visit his study. Washington designed this room to give himself a quiet space in the busy, noisy household.

At his desk, he handled the paperwork of running the estate—paying bills, ordering supplies, planning his gardens. He also wrote letters to other American leaders, expressing his ideas for the nation's future.

The study contains some of Washington's favorite possessions. A portrait of Lawrence, his beloved half brother, hangs on one wall. Near a window there is a fan chair, something that Washington especially liked. As he sat in the chair and worked a pedal, a fan above his head created a cooling breeze.

The second story contains six bedrooms. The Lafayette bedroom is named for Washington's friend, who slept there on his last visit to Mount Vernon in 1784.

Nelly Custis used the bedroom that bears her name. She married at Mount Vernon in 1799. The baby's crib in the room today was a gift to Nelly from Martha Washington when Nelly's first child was born.

A private stairway rises from the first floor to the Washingtons' bedchamber. Just as George had his study, Martha used this bedroom as her headquarters for managing the household. The room contains her desk and portraits she liked.

After Washington died, Martha no longer wished to sleep in the room that they had shared. She moved into a smaller bedroom on the third floor. Today that room holds the trunk that Martha packed for her winters with George during the war.

The Mount Vernon Ladies' Association has collected many of the Washingtons' possessions over the years. It would be impossible for visitors to see all of them as they tour the house. For this reason, the association created a museum on Mount Vernon's grounds. Inside the museum, people can admire the detail in Martha Washington's jewelry or in the handles of George Washington's swords. They can take a close look at a clay bust of George Washington.

There are many other buildings on Mount Vernon's grounds. Most are workplaces and quarters for the slaves and small houses for the paid workers. In the smokehouse, meats were cooked over smoke and preserved. Washerwomen in the washhouse scrubbed Mount Vernon's large piles of laundry. Workers in the stable cared for Washington's horses.

One service building housed the kitchen, where cooks prepared the family's meals over an open fire. Today the kitchen contains items similar to those used long ago—heavy metal pans, bright copper ladles for spooning soups and sauces, a marble pestle for grinding corn or other grains.

    The spinning house was another busy place. There, slaves used spinning wheels to turn flax into thread. Weavers later wove the thread to make linen cloth. The spinning house also served as quarters for some of the paid workers.

    Some of the house slaves lived in quarters attached to Mount Vernon's greenhouse. The Washingtons provided their slaves with what they needed to live and work, and little more. The house slaves slept in plain wooden bunks and sat on hard stools and benches. They often slept, cooked, and ate in a single room. They received rations of food, but often added to these by growing gardens, raising chickens, fishing, and hunting.

    Slaves were born on the estate, married, and raised families there, where they also grew old, died, and were buried. In 1929, the Mount Vernon Ladies' Association placed a monument to Mount Vernon's slaves on the site of their burial

The memorial to Washington's slaves

ground. A new and larger memorial stands on the site today. This simple marker bears the words Hope, Faith, and Love. Visitors often spend a quiet moment at this memorial as they remember all of the African Americans who lived in slavery, at Mount Vernon and elsewhere.

It is a short walk from the memorial to George Washington's tomb. Inside the brick family vault, marble caskets hold the remains of George and Martha Washington. This is not

Washington's original burial site. His family moved his remains to this tomb in 1831.

When people tour George Washington's home, they can imagine how he lived during his lifetime. He was a great general, the nation's first president, and a man who took delight in his home and family. At his tomb, away from the trappings of 18th-century life, people see Washington as a man for all time. Americans continue to honor the ideals for which he fought. The government he helped to create continues to protect their rights. Mount Vernon keeps the memory of Washington alive.

A bust of Washington by the French sculptor Houdon

MOUNT VERNON: A HISTORICAL TIME LINE

1732 George Washington is born at Popes Creek Farm in Westmoreland County, Virginia, to Augustine and Mary Washington.

1735 Augustine and Mary Washington move to the Little Hunting Creek Plantation with their children.

1739 The Washingtons move to Ferry Farm, near Fredericksburg, Virginia.

1740 Augustine Washington deeds the Little Hunting Creek Plantation to his oldest son, Lawrence. Lawrence Washington begins to build a new, two-story house on the site and names the estate Mount Vernon.

1743 Augustine Washington dies. Lawrence Washington marries Anne Fairfax.

1751 Lawrence Washington becomes ill with tuberculosis. George Washington travels with him to Barbados, in the West Indies.

1752 Lawrence Washington returns to Virginia and dies at Mount Vernon. George Washington begins his military service.

1754 Washington leases Mount Vernon from Lawrence's widow, Anne.

1755 Washington serves as an aide to General Edward Braddock in the French and Indian War.

1758 Washington adds a third story to the house and

redecorates its interior.

1759 George Washington and Martha Dandridge Custis are married. They settle at Mount Vernon with Martha's two children.

1761 Washington inherits Mount Vernon following the death of Lawrence's widow, Anne.

1773 Washington plans to enlarge his home.

1774 The First Continental Congress meets in Philadelphia.

1775 The American Revolution begins; the Second Continental Congress elects Washington as commander of the Continental army.

1781 Lord Cornwallis surrenders to Washington at Yorktown, Virginia; the Revolution ends. John Custis dies; his daughter and son, Nelly Custis and George Washington Parke Custis, come to live at Mount Vernon.

1783 Washington resigns as commander of the Continental forces and returns to Mount Vernon.

1787 Washington presides over the Constitutional Convention in Philadelphia. The remodeling of Mount Vernon is completed.

1789 Washington is elected president of the United States.

1797 Washington retires from the presidency.

1799	George Washington dies.
1802	Martha Washington dies; Bushrod Washington inherits Mount Vernon.
1829	Bushrod Washington dies, and Mount Vernon passes to John Augustine Washington.
1831	The bodies of George and Martha Washington are moved to a new tomb on the grounds of Mount Vernon.
1832	John Augustine Washington dies; his widow and children continue to live at Mount Vernon.
1850	John Augustine Washington, Jr., takes possession of Mount Vernon.
1853	Ann Pamela Cunningham of South Carolina founds the Mount Vernon Ladies' Association of the Union.
1858	The Mount Vernon Ladies' Association purchases Mount Vernon. The estate is opened to the public. Restoration work begins.
1861-1865	The Civil War years. Mount Vernon is the only neutral ground in the war between the North and the South.
1929	The Mount Vernon Ladies' Association places a monument to Mount Vernon's slaves on the site of their burial ground.
1939	King George VI of England visits Mount Vernon.

1974 The United States government establishes Piscataway National Park on the Maryland shore of the Potomac River, forever protecting Mount Vernon's view.

1980 Computer analysis of paint samples reveals the true colors of Mount Vernon's walls.

1983 A new monument to Mount Vernon's slaves is unveiled.

1991 Queen Elizabeth II visits Mount Vernon.

Visitor Information

Hours

9:00 A.M. to 5:00 P.M., March through October.

9:00 A.M. to 4:00 P.M., November through February.

Mount Vernon is open every day of the year.

Admission

$7 for adults.

$3 for children ages 6 through 11 when accompanied by an adult.

$6 for people age 62 and older with identification.

Tours

Mount Vernon is open for self-guided touring. Guides answer visitors' questions as they tour the mansion.

Special Events

From December 1 through January 6, special exhibits show visitors how the Washingtons entertained during the holiday season.

On Presidents' Day (the third Monday in February) at 10:00 A.M., a representative of the president of the United States lays a wreath at George Washington's tomb.

Additional information can be obtained from:

Mount Vernon Ladies' Association
Mount Vernon, VA 22121
(703) 780-2000

Index

African Americans, 63
Alexandria, Virginia, 19
Americans, 8, 15, 31, 33, 38, 65
Arlington House, 47

Barbados, 20
Bastille, 58
Bermuda, 7, 20
Bill of Rights, 38
Blue Ridge Mountains, 19
Bolton, Francis P., 50, 52
Boston, Massachusetts 31
Braddock, General Edward, 24-25
British army, 8
British navy, 15
British soldiers, 25, 31, 33

Caribbean, 15
Charleston Mercury, 44
Chesapeake Bay, 7
Civil War, 46
Concord, Massachusetts, 31
Congress, 35, 38
Constitutional Convention, 35
Continental Congress, 31
Craik, Dr. James, 40
Cunningham, Ann Pamela, 44-47, 52
Cunningham, Louisa, 43, 44
Custis, George Washington Parke (Jacky's son), 34, 47
Custis, Jacky (Martha's son), 27, 34
Custis, Nelly (Jacky's daughter), 34, 58, 60
Custis, Patsy (Martha's daughter), 27

Elizabeth II, Queen of England, 53
England, 8, 15, 21, 22, 23, 24, 28, 29, 33, 34, 48
English government, 29

English soldiers, 25
Europe, 53
Everett, Edward, 45

Ferry Farm, 15, 22
Fort Necessity, 21
France, 24
French and Indian War, 24
French Revolution, 58

George III, King of England, 31
George IV, King of England, 53
Germany, 53

House of Burgesses, 25, 27

Indians, 25

Lafayette, Marquis de, 47-48, 58
Lake Erie, 21
L'Enfant, Pierre Charles, 38
Little Hunting Creek Plantation, 14
Lord Cornwallis, 33
Lord Fairfax, 17

Mount Vernon: annual number of tourists at, 13, 55; bedrooms, 59-60; the bowling green, 28, 55; colonnades, 55; construction and enlargement of, 23, 27-29, 33-35, 40; courtyard, 55; decaying of, 42-43; dining room, 55, 57; during Civil War, 46; family vault at, 41, 63; kitchen, 61; as a memorial site, 11; museum of, 61; naming of, 16; possession of John Augustine Washington, Jr., 42; proximity to Washington D.C., 38; restoration of, 11, 45, 47-50, 52; as retirement home to George Washington, 34, 38-39; sale of,

45; slave monument on grounds of, 62-63; slavery at, 13, 16, 28, 50, 57, 61-63; smokehouse, 61; spinning house, 62; stable, 61; study, 59-60; washhouse, 61
Mount Vernon Ladies' Association, 45-48, 50, 60-62

Nazi army, 63
New World, 24
New York City, New York, 37
North Carolina, 7

Ohio, 50
Ohio River, 21

Philadelphia, Pennsylvania, 31, 34, 37
Piscataway National Park, 52
Potomac River, 7, 11, 13, 19, 33, 38, 42-43

Revolutionary War, 57

Secretary of Congress, 37
Shenandoah Valley, 19
South Carolina, 43
Spain, 15
Supreme Court, 35

Thomson, Charles (Secretary of Congress), 37
Tracy, Sarah, 45-46
Troy, New York, 45

United States of America, 9, 37, 45, 53
United States Constitution, 9, 35, 38
United States Government, 35, 42

Vernon, Admiral Edward, 16

Virginia, 7, 15, 17, 20-21, 23, 25, 43, 47

Washington, Anne (Lawrence's wife), 16-17, 22, 27
Washington, Augustine (George Washington's father), 14, 16
Washington, D.C., 11, 38
Washington, George: birthday of, 14; childhood of, 14, 15; clay bust of, 61; as a country gentleman, 25; death of, 11, 41, 47, 55, 60; education of, 15-17; favorite breakfast of, 39; as first president of U.S., 9, 37-38, 55, 65; as a gardener/farmer, 11, 16, 23, 24, 34, 40, 49; marriage of, 27; military career of, 8, 9, 20, 21, 22, 24-25, 31-33, 65; monument to, 11; as president of the Constitutional Convention, 35; retirement of, 34, 37-39; as a surveyor, 17, 19-20; as a teenager, 17, 20; tomb of, 63, 65
Washington, John Augustine Jr. (family member), 42-45
Washington, Lawrence (George's half-brother), 7-9, 15-17, 20, 22, 27, 59
Washington, Lund (George's cousin), 33
Washington, Martha Custis (George's wife), 9, 27, 32, 34, 37, 40-42, 57-58, 60, 63
Washington, Mary (George's mother), 14, 17
West Indies, 16, 20
Williamsburg, Virginia, 25, 27, 28

Yorktown, Virginia, 33